A BOOK ABOUT COLOR

Mark Gonyea

Henry Holt and Company • New York

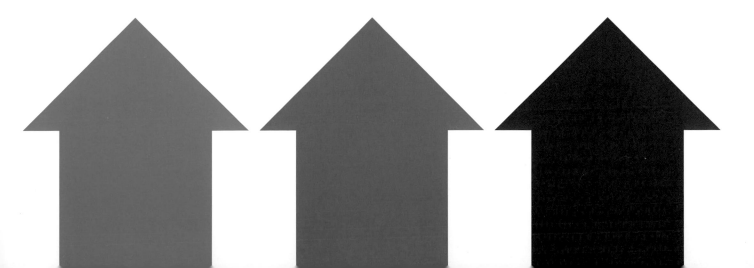

Henry Holt and Company, LLC
Publishers since 1866
175 Fifth Avenue
New York, New York 10010
www.HenryHoltKids.com

Library of Congress Control Number: 2009927639
ISBN 978-0-8050-9055-0

First Edition—2010
Printed in June 2010 in China by Macmillan Production (Asia) Ltd.,
Kwun Tong, Kowloon, Hong Kong (Supplier Code 10), on acid-free paper. ∞

3 5 7 9 10 8 6 4 2

This book is dedicated to

_____

(Your name here. Congratulations!)

Chapter One

Welcome to the Neighborhood

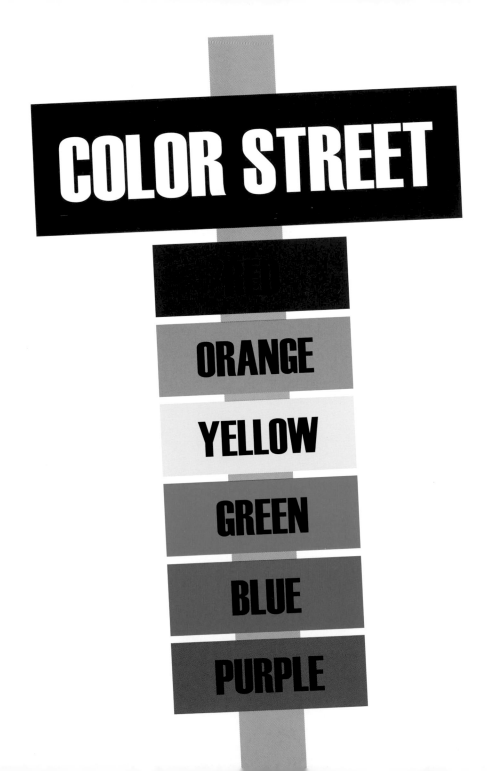

This is Color Street.

On Color Street, the houses are red, orange, yellow, green, blue, and purple.

Red, yellow, and blue
are called primary colors.
Let's make those houses bigger.

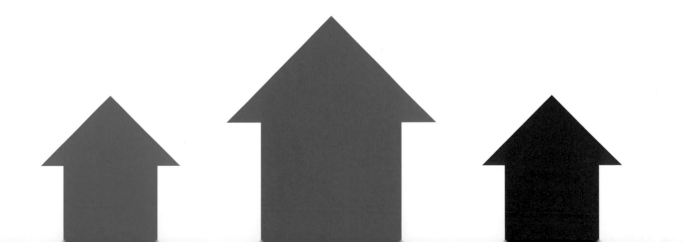

You can use the three primary colors to make more colors.

Red and yellow make orange.

Yellow and blue make green.

Blue and red make purple.

Orange, green, and purple are secondary colors because they're made with primary colors.

Chapter Two

Orange You Happy to See Me

Different colors can
mean different things.

Red is loving.

Red is
dangerous.

Orange is cheerful.

Orange is powerful.

Yellow **is warm.**

Yellow **is fun.**

Green is natural.

Green is lucky.

Blue is calm.

Blue is wet.

Purple is royal.

Purple is magical.

Chapter Three

It's Cool to Be Blue

There are warm colors,
and there are cool colors.

Green, blue, and purple
are cool colors.

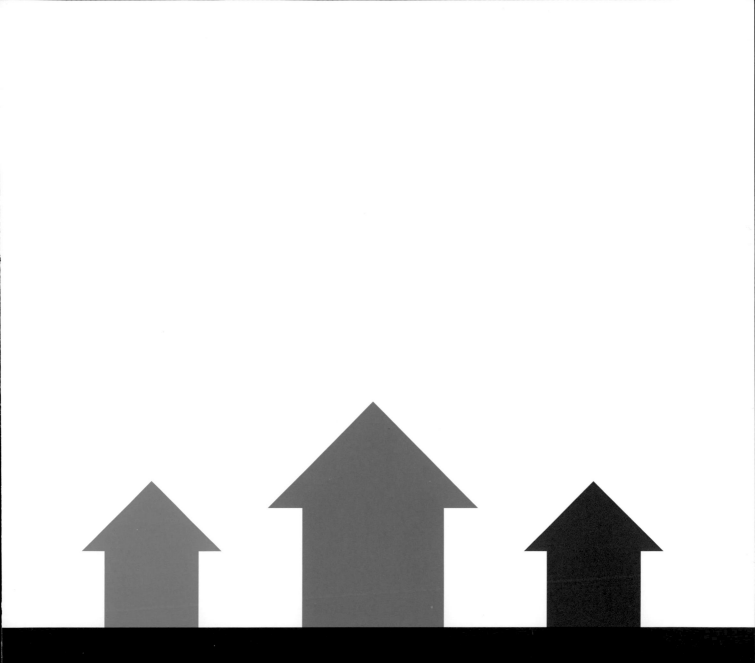

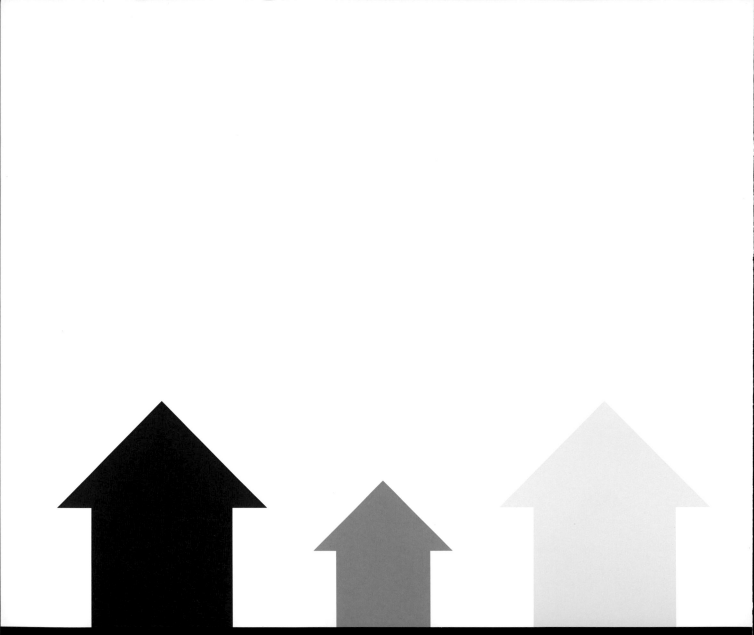

Red, orange, and yellow
are warm colors.

Cool colors recede,
or move to the back.

Warm colors rise
to the front.

Chapter Four

What a Lovely Shade of Green You Are!

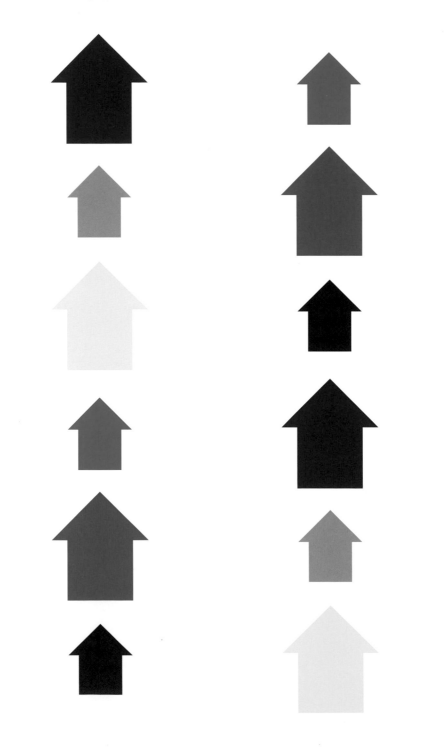

Color Street has two sides.
Red and green, orange and blue,
and yellow and purple are across
from each other.

These color pairs are called
complementary, which means
they work well together.

Like so.

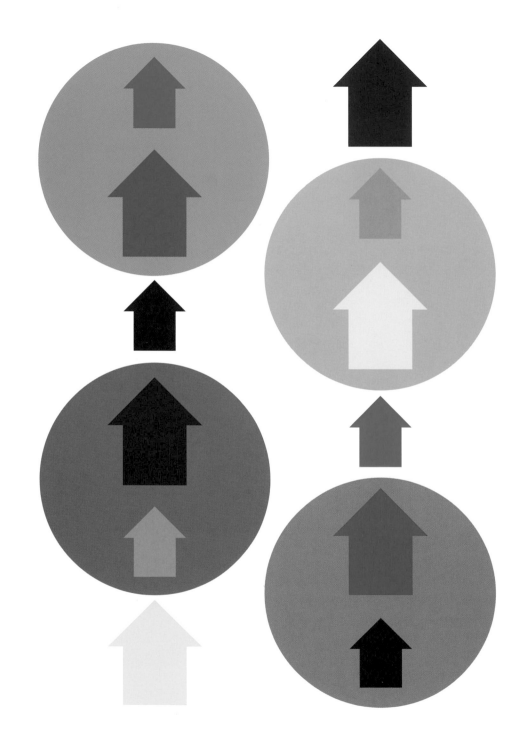

Colors next to each
other on Color Street
are called analogous.

Pretty fancy word for
"next to."

Analogous colors are harmonious and work well together.

You can also mix analogous colors to get new colors, like red-orange, and orange-yellow.

Chapter Five

Deep Purple

Saturation is the amount
of color in . . . well . . . color.

Desaturation means
less color is being used and
colors become paler.

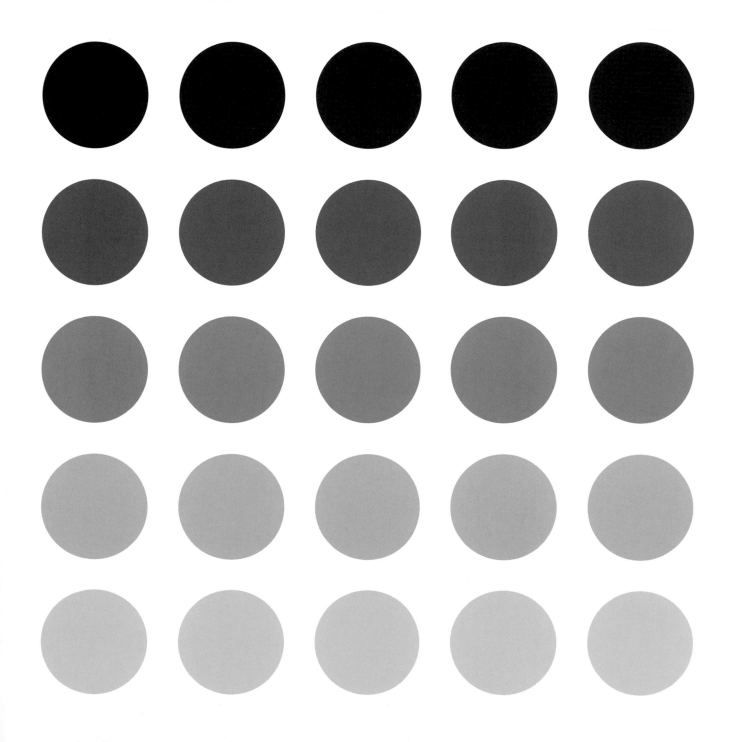

Very saturated colors
are vibrant and exciting.

Less saturated colors are
faded and not as vibrant.

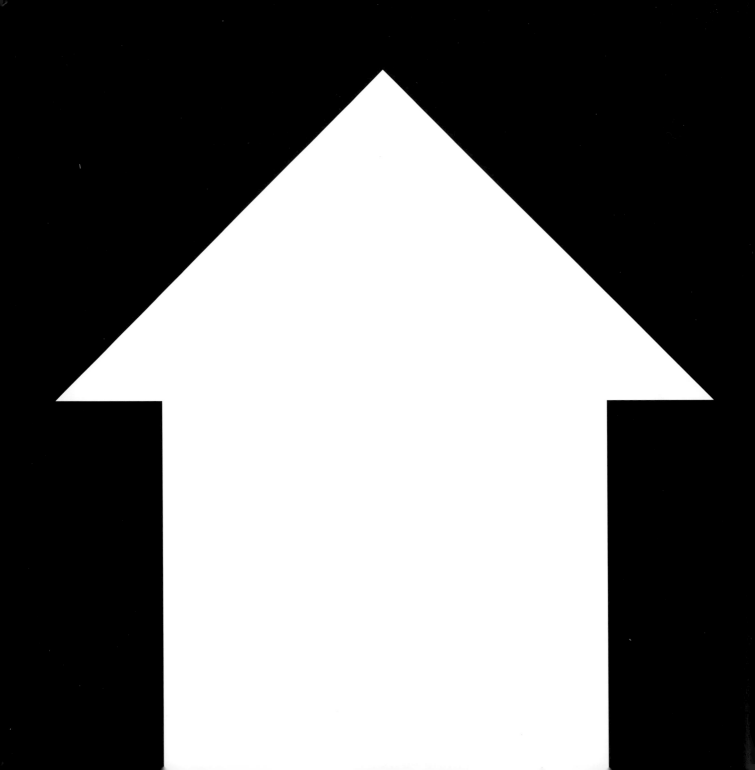

Chapter Six

Hey! Did You Forget
About Black and White?
Well, I Didn't!

White is
the absence
of color.

Black is all the colors together.

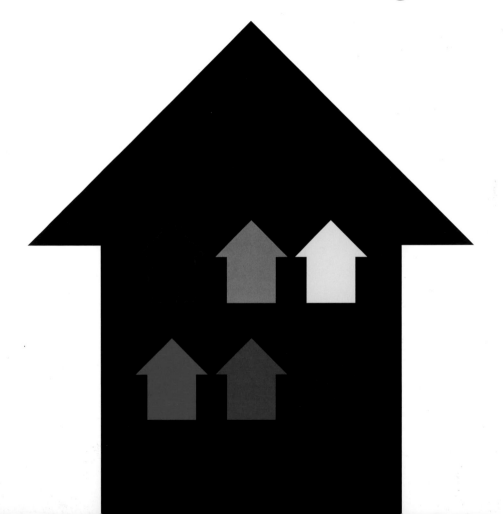

White is pure.

White is clean.

Black is
mysterious.

Black is sophisticated.

When black or white
is added, colors become
darker or lighter. That's called
changing the value.

Lighter values have more
white and can make things
seem friendly and soft.

Darker values have
more black and can make things
seem creepy and menacing.

The Last Chapter

Putting It All Together

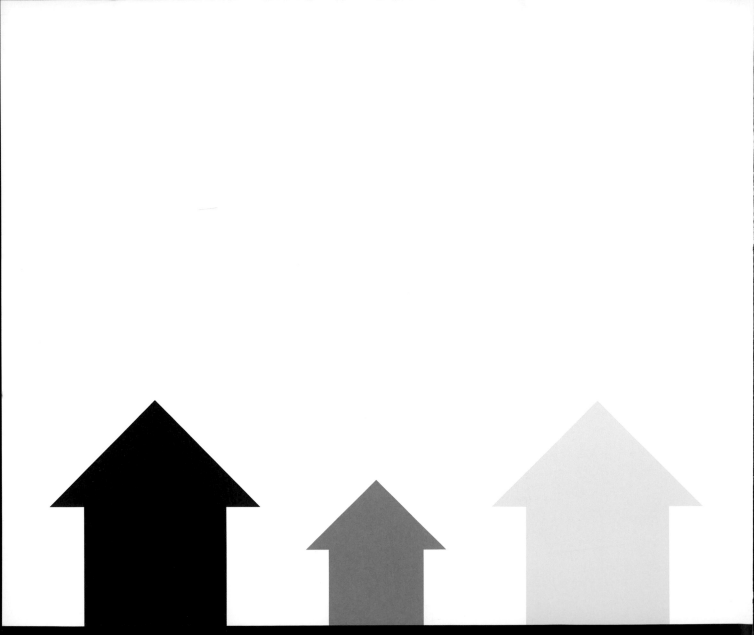

We've been up and down Color Street, but now let's see it from a new perspective.

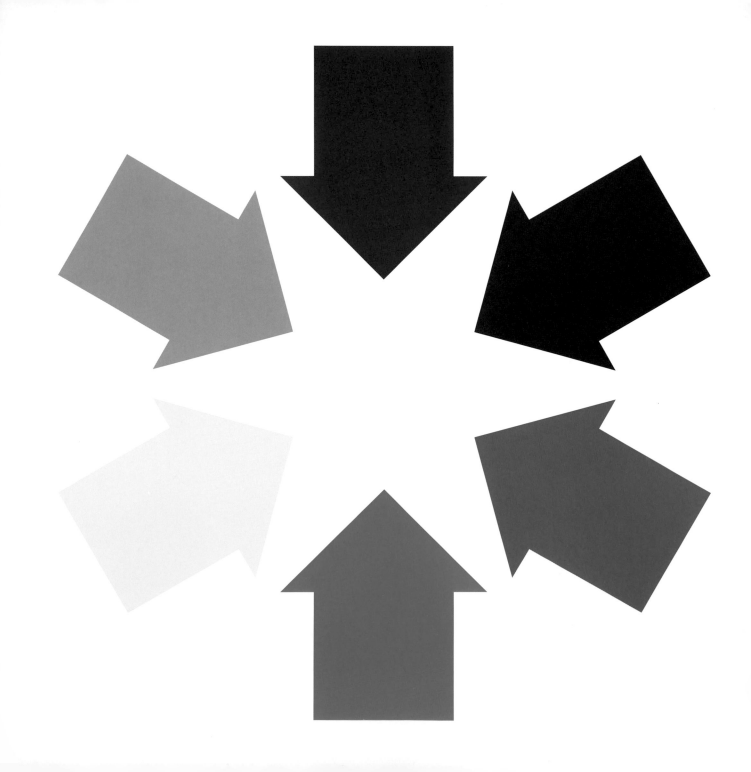

Imagine the houses
are arranged in a circle.

Doesn't it look like
a wheel now?

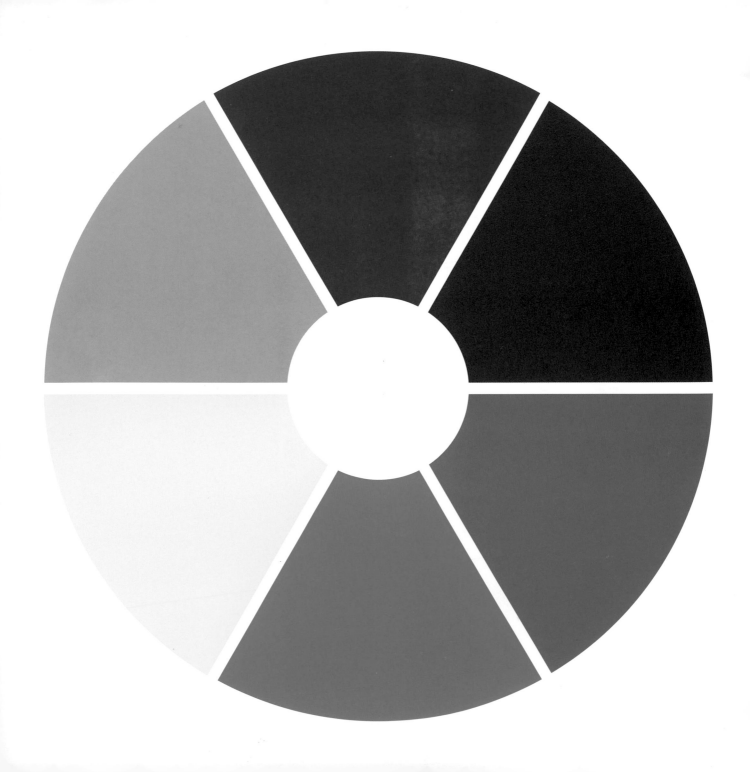

It still has primary colors
and secondary colors.

It has complementary
colors across from each other,
and analogous colors next
to each other.

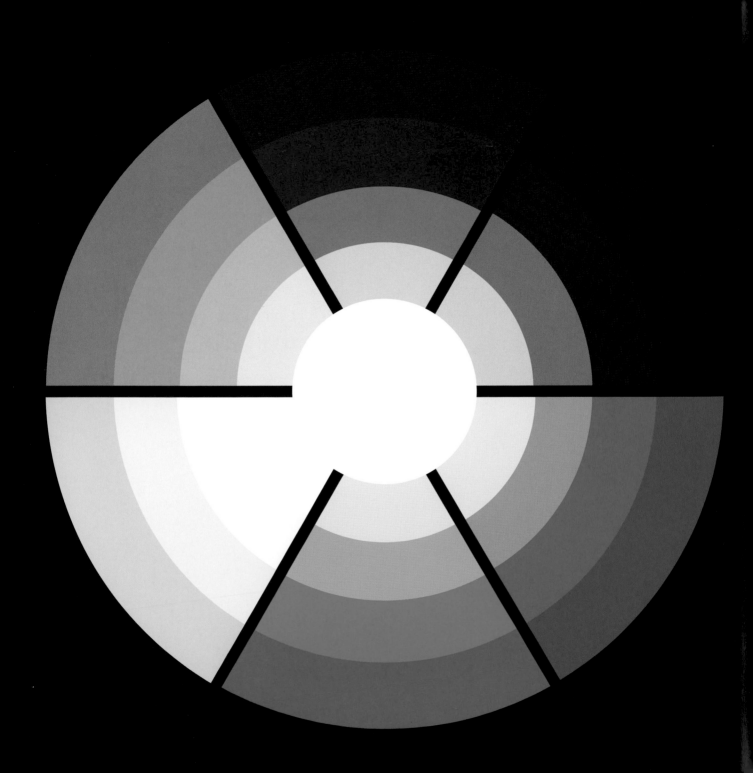

It has warm and cool colors.

It has values and saturation.

This is called the color wheel,
and all kinds of artists use it
to choose colors and visualize
how they go together.

Where on Color Street
will you use it to go?